CW01512520

Original title:
Dappled Wisps Over the Elf Hash

Author: Sara Säde
ISBN HARDBACK: 978-1-80562-960-3
ISBN PAPERBACK: 978-1-80564-481-1

Laughter of the Spirits at Dusk

In the twilight's tender embrace,
Whispers dance on the breeze,
Echoes of laughter fill the air,
As shadows dip beneath the trees.

The stars twinkle with knowing grace,
Mischief glimmers in their light,
Spirits frolic through the glen,
Chasing dreams into the night.

A symphony of nightingale song,
Melodies woven with delight,
The world sighs in sweet repose,
Under the watch of the moonlight.

Crickets chirp with playful glee,
A tapestry spun with mirth,
Nature hums a gentle tune,
Celebrating life and rebirth.

So gather close, let laughter ring,
As dusk drapes its velvet shroud,
With spirits soaring, hearts alive,
In the twilight, we're all avowed.

Mystical Radiance Among the Blossoms

In the garden where secrets bloom,
Petals whisper tales of old,
Wings flutter in the fragrant air,
Where mysteries gently unfold.

Beneath the boughs of ancient trees,
Sunbeams spill, a golden hue,
Each blossom holds a spark of light,
A promise born anew.

Fairies twirl in shimmering veils,
Dancing on the dewy grass,
Their laughter mingles with the breeze,
In a world where moments pass.

The blooms exchange their heartfelt dreams,
In hues of pink and azure bright,
Within this realm of wonder vast,
Awaits a journey through the night.

So pause, dear friend, and take it in,
This mystical radiance so rare,
Among the blossoms, let us tread,
And join the magic hovering there.

Secrets Entwined in Nature's Veil

In the forest where shadows play,
Nature's secrets softly sigh,
Each leaf a tale, each root a song,
In whispers only trees imply.

The brook babbles in tender tones,
Telling stories of days gone by,
Where echoes of enchantment dwell,
Beneath the watchful, azure sky.

Moss-kissed stones, their patience worn,
Guard the dreams of those long past,
With every breeze that stirs the air,
A legacy forever cast.

Flowers bloom in vibrant hues,
Wrapped in mysteries, soft and slight,
The petals hold the laughter shared,
Of sunlit days and starlit nights.

So wander through this veil of green,
And listen close with open heart,
For nature speaks in spoken breath,
And every whisper plays a part.

Luminous Secrets of Starlit Glens

In glens where shadows softly dance,
The stars weave tales in whispered chance.
A silver sheen on blades of grass,
Holding secrets, time shall pass.

The moon, a guardian up so high,
Watches over the night's soft sigh.
With every glimmer, dreams take flight,
Embraced in magic, cloaked in light.

Swaying Foliage Under the Veil of Night

In swaying boughs, a gentle sway,
The leaves converse in soft ballet.
A lullaby of rustling sounds,
Where mystery in silence bounds.

The darkness wraps like velvet threads,
As twilight hums, the earth now beds.
With whispered breaths, the night reveals,
The tender heart of how it feels.

Enigma of the Woodland Spirits

In woods where ancient echoes play,
The spirits dance at end of day.
With gossamer wings, they weave their song,
A melody of right and wrong.

With every rustle and soft glance,
They beckon forth to join the dance.
A tale unfolds in nature's light,
Where shadows shimmer, pure delight.

Flickering Lights Beneath Canopy Skies

Beneath the canopy of leafy dreams,
The flickering lights share silent themes.
A tapestry of night unfurls,
As laughter from the starlit whirls.

Each flicker tells of stories past,
Of fleeting time, and shadows cast.
In every bright and tender gleam,
A world awaits within a dream.

Glimmers of Magic in Sylvan Spaces

In twilight's glow, the shadows dance,
Whispers weave a silent trance.
Mossy carpets, emerald green,
Secrets held in spaces unseen.

Fireflies twinkle, a gentle light,
Guiding dreams into the night.
Ancient oaks wear crowns of lore,
Guarding tales of yore and more.

Underneath the starry dome,
Each creature finds its hidden home.
Mysteries linger in the air,
Dancing softly, wild and rare.

A breeze like silk through branches weaves,
Magic spins in silver leaves.
The hidden paths begin to call,
Echoing spells within the thrall.

In these woods, the heart awakes,
A fleeting glance, the world remakes.
Glimmers calling, soft and sweet,
In sylvan spaces, magic meets.

Secrets of the Fey Beneath Starry Canopies

Beneath the stars, the fey do tread,
Where moonlight kisses, softly spread.
Delicate creatures, laughter bright,
Guard the secrets of the night.

Shimmering wings in twilight's gleam,
Filling hearts with wildest dream.
Elfin songs on gentle breeze,
Whisper magic through the trees.

In hidden glades, the shadows play,
Where twilight melts to dusk and sway.
A dance of light, a fleeting sigh,
The feyling's whispers float on high.

Rivers flow with stories old,
Tales of glory quietly told.
In fragrant blooms of nightfall's grace,
The fey weave spells in soft embrace.

Secrets hidden, truths untold,
In starry canopies unfold.
Beneath the moon's enchanting glow,
The heart of magic starts to grow.

Ethereal Veils in the Heart of the Woods

Veils of mist in morning's light,
Shroud the woods in dreams and flight.
Echoes linger, soft and rare,
Whispers drift on fragrant air.

Curtains drawn by nature's hand,
Reveal a world where dreams can stand.
Where every tree has tales to share,
And creatures pause, as if aware.

A patch of flowers, colors bold,
Beneath green arms, a story told.
Glimmers flicker, shimmer and fade,
In this enchanted, secret glade.

Footsteps softly on the ground,
Nature's heartbeat, a gentle sound.
Hidden pathways beckon still,
Drawn to wonders, feel the thrill.

Ethereal veils, a soft embrace,
In the heart of woods, find your place.
Mysteries weave, as spirits glide,
In this realm where shadows hide.

Celestial Echoes through Verdant Halls

In verdant halls where echoes play,
Celestial whispers guide the way.
Nature's chorus, a soothing song,
Inviting hearts where they belong.

An ancient tree, its branches sway,
Holding dreams of yesterday.
Underneath its timeless guise,
A world awakens, magic flies.

With every step on mossy floor,
Legends linger just beyond the door.
Tales of starlight, shadows bright,
Dance together in the night.

Through hidden glens where fairies tread,
Every rustle, every thread.
Binding worlds that time forgot,
Magic lives in every spot.

Celestial echoes, sweet and clear,
Draw the wanderer ever near.
In verdant halls where dreams ignite,
The heart finds peace in pure delight.

Luminescent Dreams on a Sylvan Breeze

In twilight hours, dreams take flight,
Beneath the stars, a gleaming sight.
Whispers dance on leaves so green,
In the hush of night, they weave a sheen.

A shimmer bright upon the brook,
Nature's magic, a secret nook.
The air alive with tales untold,
In softest hues of blue and gold.

Flickering lights like fireflies gleam,
Carrying wonders of every dream.
Touched by glimmers from above,
Wrapped in whispers of endless love.

Each petal glows with a mystic charm,
Safe and warm in nature's arm.
Breezes carry the night's sweet song,
A lullaby where we belong.

So wander forth, let your heart see,
In luminescent dreams we flee.
For here in shadows, light ignites,
Guiding us through enchanted nights.

Enigmatic Lights Beneath Leafy Canopies

In secret groves where shadows play,
Mysterious lights lead us astray.
Beneath the boughs of ancient trees,
Whispers twine with the gentle breeze.

Glimmers wink through emerald leaves,
Spinning tales that the heart believes.
With every step, a soft intrigue,
Enticing us to seek and league.

The air shimmers with unspoken lore,
As echoes beckon from days of yore.
Paths untrodden, dreams unfold,
In every corner, wonders bold.

Dancing lights, a spectral veil,
Guide us through this mystical trail.
A journey borne on nature's breath,
Where life and magic dance with death.

So linger here, let time be slow,
Under leafy canopies aglow.
Find joy in secrets that weave and twine,
In enigmatic lights, our spirits shine.

Ghostly Glimmers in the Forest's Embrace

In forest depths, where whispers reign,
Ghostly glimmers softly wane.
Echoes of footfalls linger near,
As shadows draw us, calm yet clear.

A silken glow on moss-carpeted ground,
Brings life to dreams that once were bound.
Hushed serenades of the night wind,
Gently calling to minds unpinned.

In the twilight, shadows entwine,
Fleeting figures, seraphic sign.
With every flicker, a tale relays,
In the dark woods, lost in a haze.

Light dances softly on starlit trails,
Cascading whispers, the heart exhales.
In this embrace of ghosts so bright,
We find our peace in the enveloping night.

So let us wander beneath moon's gaze,
In ghostly glimmers, our spirits blaze.
For in these woods where stars converge,
The magic calls, and dreams emerge.

Twilight Reflections in Elven Nooks

In elven nooks, where twilight sighs,
Reflections dance in amber skies.
Rivers flow with secrets old,
Carrying whispers that the night holds.

Beneath the willows, shadows blend,
Where tales of wonder never end.
A flicker here, a sparkle there,
Elven magic fills the air.

Time and space feel light as air,
As moonbeams play without a care.
Every heart knows the ancient song,
In twilight's embrace, we all belong.

Stars awaken in velvet skies,
Offering glimpses of the wise.
In these nooks, our dreams align,
In a world where magic is divine.

So pause and breathe in the night's glow,
As twilight reflections begin to flow.
In elven realms, let spirits soar,
With every heartbeat, we seek for more.

Celestial Freckles on the Forest Floor

In twilight's grasp, the shadows dance,
A sprinkle of stars in nature's expanse.
Each leaf adorned with silver light,
Whispers of magic in the cool of night.

Underneath the oaks, the secrets lie,
Beneath the moon's soft, watchful eye.
A tapestry woven from dreams and lore,
Celestial freckles, forevermore.

Each footstep taken on this sacred ground,
Echoes of stories in silence found.
Nature's verses sing to the heart,
In this enchanted realm, none shall part.

The glow of fireflies paints the air,
A lingering message, a gentle prayer.
When night unfurls her velvet cloak,
In every shadow, life awoke.

So tread with care, dear wandering soul,
For the forest whispers, makes you whole.
In each star's twinkle, a tale now springs,
Celestial freckles, the joy that brings.

Luminous Secrets of the Ancient Path

Along the winding, ancient way,
Lies history in the light of day.
Moss-covered stones tell tales of old,
Luminous secrets waiting to unfold.

The air is thick with forgotten dreams,
Where sunlight dances, and magic gleams.
With each soft step on the forest trail,
Echoes of wonder begin to unveil.

Can you hear the whispers in the breeze?
They carry whispers of old, ancient trees.
Rooted in wisdom, they stand so tall,
Guardians of stories, answering the call.

Beneath the twilight, shadows entwine,
As time stands still in the soft moonshine.
Nature cradles every regret,
In luminous secrets, we'll never forget.

So follow the path where wonders gleam,
In the heart of the forest, chase the dream.
For every twist and turn may impart,
A glimpse of magic that stirs the heart.

Ethereal Breaths of the Whispering Woods

In the heart of the woods where the silence sighs,
Ethereal breaths weave through the skies.
With every rustle, a story spins,
The dance of shadows, the tale begins.

Leaves murmur secrets of days gone by,
Wisdom flows gently, as the ages fly.
In dappled light, the spirits sway,
Among the whispers, lost fears fray.

The brook sings softly, a melodic tune,
Cradled in dusk, beneath the glowing moon.
Each ripple a promise, a tale to share,
In the arms of nature, free from care.

As twilight deepens, the magic stirs,
Shimmering echoes where the night occurs.
In the quiet shadows, the heart shall find,
Ethereal breaths, entangled and blind.

So linger a while in the twilight haze,
Embrace the stories, the night's soft gaze.
For in the whispers of the woods so deep,
Are dreams awakened, and memories to keep.

Starry Eyes of the Forest Guardians

Amidst the ancient trees, they reside,
Starry eyes that watch and bide.
From roots to crown, their wisdom flows,
The forest guardians, in twilight glows.

Each glimmering gaze holds tales untold,
Of life and loss, of the brave and bold.
With branches wide, they cradle the night,
In every whisper, a flickering light.

In moonlit glades, their laughter sings,
As stars alight on silvery wings.
Through shadows long and paths unseen,
The guardians watch, both fierce and keen.

Through storms and sun, they stand their ground,
In every heartbeat, a solace found.
So listen closely, for you might hear,
The ancient wisdom drawing near.

In unity with earth, they're never alone,
For in the wild, they've made their home.
With starry eyes, they guard our dreams,
With every rustle, hope redeems.

Resonance of Light in the Nature Realm

In the forest where the whispering trees,
Sunbeams dance on the leaves with ease.
Crystal waters shimmer with delight,
Nature sings under the radiant light.

Flowers bloom with colors so bright,
Every petal catches the soft sunlight.
Winds carry stories from afar,
Soft echoes resonate like a gentle star.

The mountains rise with majesty grand,
Guardians of secrets in this enchanted land.
Birds take flight on whispering wings,
In the presence of magic, the heart sings.

Beneath the boughs, shadows play,
Nature embraces the end of day.
With each heartbeat, life intertwines,
In this realm where the soul defines.

So cherish the light in the nature realm,
Where every creature finds a helm.
In the beauty of each fleeting glance,
Let your spirit join in the dance.

Fleeing Phantoms of the Shade

In twilight's grasp, the shadows creep,
Phantoms whisper secrets deep.
Through the mist, they twist and swirl,
Elusive forms in a ghostly whirl.

Lost in memories, they softly fade,
Chasing dreams where the night is made.
With every step, the darkness sighs,
A haunting melody beneath starlit skies.

They beckon softly, like a fading tune,
Lost in the embrace of a silver moon.
Footsteps echo on the forest floor,
As whispers call from the unseen shore.

Yet in the fear of shadows' hold,
Courage blooms in hearts so bold.
For with each phantom that we flee,
A light emerges, wild and free.

So dance with courage against the night,
Though phantoms linger, seek the light.
In every shadow, let hope ignite,
And weave your dreams into the night.

Golden Flecks in the Glooming Wild

Amidst the dark where the wild winds sigh,
Golden flecks of wonder fly.
Softly glimmering in the night,
A sprinkle of magic, a pure delight.

Beneath the cloak of starry skies,
Fireflies flicker and close their eyes.
In the gloom, their dance unfolds,
Stories of ancient time retold.

Secrets hidden within the bark,
Whispers of life in the forest dark.
Every rustle, a promise made,
In the heart of the woods, courage displayed.

So wander deep where shadows play,
Embrace the night, let it sway.
For even in darkness, light may hide,
In golden flecks, let your spirit glide.

With every step on the wild terrain,
Gather the moments, let joy remain.
In the gloaming where wonders steal,
Find the magic that you can feel.

Flashes of Grace in the Inhabited Wood

In the woods where enchantment thrives,
Flashes of grace in life's great archives.
Creatures weave tales through the trees,
As whispers ride on the gentle breeze.

Sunlight dapples the forest floor,
Each moment a gift that we can explore.
With every step, stories unfold,
Of melodies sung and legends told.

Through the thickets, the heart takes flight,
In the embrace of nature, pure delight.
Here, every shadow tells a tale,
Of love and loss, of winds that sail.

As twilight paints the sky with grace,
Hearts awaken, finding their place.
In the inhabited wood, life does bloom,
Filling the air with sweet perfume.

So let your spirit wander and roam,
In the embrace of the wild, find your home.
For in the flashes of grace, you'll see,
The beauty that lives eternally.

Dreamweaver's Touch in Secret Places

In twilight's grip, where shadows play,
The dreamweaver's touch leads souls astray.
With whispers soft, they dance and glide,
In the secret places where magic hides.

A tapestry woven with threads of light,
In hidden glades, they take their flight.
Each heart a lantern, glowing bright,
Illuminating paths in the velvet night.

The sighing breeze carries tales untold,
Of treasures lost and treasures bold.
With every step on the mossy floor,
The dreamweaver calls, forevermore.

Beneath the boughs where moonlight weaves,
A sanctuary lies, where no one deceives.
In hushed tones, the forest speaks,
Of dreams and fears, of hopes it keeps.

As dawn approaches, the visions fade,
Yet memories linger in the glade.
For in the heart of the midnight hour,
The dreamweaver's magic holds its power.

Secrets of the Star-Kissed Thicket

In thickets deep, where fairies roam,
Secrets whispered, far from home.
Beneath the stars' celestial glow,
Mysteries in the moonlight flow.

Hidden paths where the gentle deer,
Glimpse the magic that draws them near.
With every rustle, the leaves confide,
The tales of the night and dreams inside.

A shimmering brook sings a quiet song,
Echoing soft where shadows belong.
In the star-kissed thicket, hearts entwine,
With whispers of the ethereal divine.

The nightingale's call, a silken thread,
Weaving through thoughts as wishes spread.
In corners sheltered, where silence reigns,
The secrets of nature, as love remains.

As dawn's brush paints the skies anew,
The secrets shared, a cherished hue.
In the thicket's depth, forever known,
The mysteries of the heart have grown.

Iridescent Veils in the Whispers of Night

Under the veil of the twilight sky,
Whispers of night unfold and sigh.
Iridescent shimmers touch the ground,
As the world is wrapped in dreams profound.

With flickering lights, the shadows play,
Guiding the lost who've lost their way.
Each breath a promise, each heartbeat a thrill,
In the whispers of night, spirits will.

Crickets serenade the darkened glen,
While the moon hums softly, again and again.
In the tranquil hush, the heart can find,
The beauty of silence, the peace of the mind.

Iridescent veils dance with grace,
In the canvas of night, they weave their place.
Stories of wonder, the stars narrate,
In the tapestry woven by love and fate.

With morning's kiss, the magic fades,
Yet within the heart, the memory wades.
For in every dream, in every sigh,
The iridescent veils never truly die.

Echoes Beneath the Canopy of Stars

Beneath the stars, a world unfolds,
Where echoes whisper secrets bold.
In the midnight hour, still and deep,
Wonders awaken from their sleep.

The ancient trees with stories lean,
Guardians of all that lies unseen.
With every rustle, a tale recites,
Of lost loves and enchanted nights.

In the glow of fireflies, magic swirls,
As dreams of adventure unfurl.
Echoes of laughter, of joy and pain,
In the Shimmering night, memories remain.

The constellations weave the fable true,
Mapping the dreams that once we knew.
In the melody of crickets' song,
The heart finds solace, where it belongs.

When dawn dips low, the echoes fade,
Yet in the heart, the dream is laid.
Beneath the stars, forever near,
The echoes of love, forever clear.

Beacons in the Heart of Enchantment

In the woods where whispers spin,
Fairy lights begin their dance.
Each flicker tells a tale,
Of dreams that drift in evanescent trance.

Beneath the boughs of ancient trees,
Heartbeats sync with midnight's song.
A shimmering path of silvered leaves,
Where magic's breath and night belong.

Stars peek shyly, glimmering bright,
Their secrets twinkling in the air.
Guiding souls through velvet night,
In every spark, a dream to share.

The fireflies weave their glowing thread,
A tapestry of hidden lore.
In their glow, the lost words tread,
Leading hearts to the enchanted shore.

In the stillness, shadows sway,
Guardian spirits whisper low.
In each heartbeat, they softly play,
Eternal magic, forever aglow.

Choreography of Shadows in the Glade

In the glade where shadows twirl,
Creatures leap with playful grace.
The moonlight bathes the world in pearl,
As whispers weave through the still space.

Branches sway, a rhythmic beat,
Nature composes her nightly song.
With every tale the nightbirds greet,
The darkness hums, so sweet and strong.

Dancers glide on velvet ground,
Each movement tells a story true.
In their steps, enchantment's found,
As dreams awaken, fresh and new.

Underneath the starry dome,
Echoes of laughter fill the night.
In this wild, enchanted home,
The shadows leap in pure delight.

With every flicker of twilight glow,
The glade transforms into a stage.
A whimsical world where wonders flow,
Where hearts ignite and spirits engage.

Mystical Glows of the Sylvan Spirit

In forests deep, where spirits play,
A shimmering light beckons near.
Mystical glows lead the way,
Whispering softly, drawing us here.

Amongst the leaves, soft echoes hum,
A symphony of nature's grace.
Where shadows dance and harmonies come,
The sylvan spirit finds its place.

Luminous orbs float above,
Guiding flutters through the night.
Cradled in warmth, like a mother's love,
They wrap the forest in gentle light.

The breeze carries tales long unsung,
From ancient trees to crystal streams.
In every heartbeat, magic's begun,
Stirring depths of forgotten dreams.

Beneath the arch of twilight's glow,
Nature sings in vibrant hues.
In every rustle, a story flows,
As time dances, we are renewed.

Serpentine Trails Through Midsummer Night

Through winding paths where wildflowers bloom,
The night unfolds with fragrant ease.
Stars emerge to banish gloom,
As moonbeams weave through swaying trees.

Serpentine trails lure the keen,
Adventurers of heart and soul.
With every step, a magic gleaned,
As shadows dance and night takes toll.

In the hush, whispers take flight,
Secrets float upon the breeze.
The enchantment swells in the still of night,
Carried forth by the dreaming leaves.

Wild creatures stir and venture near,
Eyes like jewels, glisten bright.
In their gaze, courage casts fear,
Guiding hearts on paths of light.

Through every turn, the world unfolds,
An adventure spun with ancient thread.
In midsummer's arms, our spirits hold,
To the whispers of the wild that led.

Ethereal Dreams on Twilight Wings

In twilight's glow, the shadows play,
Where whispers dance and fairies sway,
A world unseen begins to gleam,
As dreams unfold on silver stream.

With every flutter, hearts align,
As stars above begin to shine,
Each breath of night, a gentle sigh,
On twilight wings, our spirits fly.

The moonlight casts its silver thread,
On slumbering fields where visions tread,
Within the hush, our hopes ignite,
In ethereal realms, we take flight.

Soft echoes weave enchanting tales,
As time stands still, the magic sails,
Through quiet woods, with eyes aglow,
We navigate where dreamers go.

So let the night embrace your soul,
As twilight's wings make dreamers whole,
In whispered realms where magic's found,
Forever lost, forever bound.

Shimmering Fables of the Forest Path

Beneath the boughs of ancient trees,
Where stories hum upon the breeze,
Shimmering fables softly weave,
In every breath, in every leave.

A winding path of secrets calls,
Where sunlight falls and nature thralls,
With gentle rustles, tales unfold,
In whispers sweet, both brave and bold.

Each step we take, the ground aglow,
As magical wonders start to flow,
Creatures peep from hiding places,
In shimmering light, with curious faces.

The brook hums soft, a lovely song,
While shadows dance, both bright and strong,
In forests deep, where legends thrive,
In every heart, the fables dive.

So wander forth, let spirits soar,
Upon this path to tales galore,
For in the woods, where stories are,
The shimmering dreams will take you far.

Secret Scents in the Veil of Darkness

In shadows cast by moonlight pale,
Where secrets drift like sweet perfume,
The veil of darkness holds its breath,
Awash in scents of life and death.

Each whisper carries tales untold,
Of mystic quests and hearts so bold,
The air is thick with ancient lore,
In every scent, a hidden door.

Beneath the stars, the night's embrace,
Conceals a world, a secret place,
Where echoes murmur, softly call,
In fragrant dreams, we rise, we fall.

With every step, the shadows sigh,
As blooming night begins to die,
For in the dark, the magic stirs,
In secret scents, the mystery blurs.

So linger here, beneath the stars,
In darkness rich with tales from afar,
For every breath is woven tight,
In the sacred dance of day and night.

A Breath of Magic in Dusk's Embrace

As sunlight dips and day takes flight,
The dusk unfurls its cloak of night,
With every breath, the magic swells,
In whispers soft, the evening tells.

The sky is brushed with shades of gold,
In twilight's arms, the stories unfold,
A flicker here, a shimmer there,
As dreams awaken in the air.

In gentle hues, the shadows gleam,
A world alive, a vibrant dream,
Each heartbeat sounds, a pulse divine,
In dusk's embrace, our fates entwine.

With every sigh, the night breathes in,
The promise of each tale akin,
Where magic sways and stars ignite,
In dusky realms, we find our light.

So let us dance beneath the veil,
Where every moment starts to pale,
For in this breath, the magic stays,
In dusk's embrace, our hearts ablaze.

Light and Shade in the Whispering Groves

In groves where shadows softly play,
The light slips through in gentle sway.
A dance of whispers, leaves in flight,
They twinkle softly, day to night.

With every step, a story told,
Of ancient magic, treasures bold.
The sunbeams weave a golden thread,
While secrets stir beneath the spread.

The brook's laughter, bright and clear,
Calls forth the dreams we hold so dear.
In light and shade, the heart knows well,
A place where dreams and spirits dwell.

The air is thick with tales untold,
Of lovers lost and knights of old.
In every rustling, every sigh,
The groves are alive, and we can fly.

Yet even in this sacred glade,
The shadows beckon, softly made.
For light and shade are one, they say,
In whispering groves where spirits lay.

Fantasies of Light in Hidden Hollows

Beneath the boughs of twisted trees,
The hidden hollows hum with ease.
Fantasies glow in vibrant hues,
A world of wonder waits for clues.

The flickering lights in twilight's grasp,
Hold tightly to the dreams we clasp.
The fireflies dance, a sparkling sea,
Inviting hearts to wander free.

In every corner, magic glows,
Where ancient wisdom gently flows.
The echoes of enchantments past,
In whispers soft, the moments cast.

A tapestry of starry fate,
Awaits those who dare to wait.
The shadows stretch, embracing light,
In hidden hollows, pure delight.

Each nook and cranny holds a spell,
A story woven, hard to tell.
For in the quiet, dreams take flight,
In fantasies of shimmering light.

Serene Reflections along the Mystic Path

Along the path where silence reigns,
The mystic whispers, soft like chains.
Reflections shimmer in the stream,
Echoing the heart's own dream.

The gentle breeze stirs all that's seen,
Awakening thoughts, sweet and serene.
With every step, the world unfolds,
In hues of jade and marigold.

Secrets linger where shadows blend,
Telling tales of how they mend.
The light cascades on leaves so dear,
As visions dance and disappear.

The path invites, it knows the way,
Through tranquil glades, both bright and gray.
In gentle curves, we find our truth,
In serene reflections, lost in youth.

A journey etched in softest sighs,
With every turn, beneath the skies.
The mystic path holds hearts entwined,
In its embrace, all doubts unwind.

Elven Secrets Woven in the Night

Beneath the starlit canopy bright,
Elven whispers weave the night.
With silver threads and shadowed dreams,
They dance in moonlight's softest gleams.

In emerald glades where silence sings,
The echoes of old magic clings.
Each secret held, a gentle sigh,
As stardust mingles with the sky.

The night unveils its mystic lore,
Of ancient paths and hidden doors.
In shadows deep, the legends call,
Inviting all who dare to fall.

With every step, the magic flows,
Through elven hearts, the wonder grows.
In twilight's glow, the night unfolds,
As stories rich and daring bolds.

So linger where the starlight plays,
And let the dreams steal you away.
For in the night, the secrets gleam,
In elven tales where wishes dream.

A Serenade of Shadows in Woodland Nooks

In the whispering woods where the shadows play,
Leaves shimmer softly in the waning day.
Beneath the boughs where secrets thrive,
Mysteries linger; the dark come alive.

A rustle of wings, a flicker of light,
Echoes of laughter erupt in the night.
Spiders weave tales in delicate silk,
While owls lend wisdom, as smooth as milk.

Moss blankets the path in emerald hues,
As twilight unfolds her silken views.
The whispering trees sway to the sound,
Of enchantment and dreams that abound.

A flicker of starlight, a spark of glee,
Each shadowed figure dances, wild and free.
The hush of twilight, a comforting shroud,
Nurtures the magic beneath the cloud.

Among the twilight's soft, soothing sigh,
A spell is spun, where soft shadows lie.
In woodland nooks, the world stays still,
As melodies of night weave their gentle thrill.

Faerie Flickers Beneath a Starlit Dome

Under the canopy of shimmering light,
Faerie flickers dart through the night.
Whispers of magic in the cool dew air,
Dancing delight, a radiant affair.

With wings like petals kissed by dawn,
They weave through the meadows, all dusk till dawn.
Each glint and glow a twinkling tease,
Carrying dreams on the evening breeze.

Scents of wildflowers perfume the night,
Guided by stars that twinkle so bright.
The world becomes soft, as wishes take flight,
In a tapestry woven from pure delight.

Among the trees where the shadows blend,
Magic and wonder begin and never end.
The faeries giggle, their laughter rings,
In a night where enchantment forever clings.

Under the starlit dome so wide,
The ethereal dance, no reason to hide.
In every flicker, a story unfurls,
Within the heart of these enchanted pearls.

Enchanted Drifts in the Realm of Whimsy

In realms where whimsy whispers and twirls,
A tapestry woven of fantastical pearls.
With colors that shimmer, a vibrant sight,
Every corner hides a spark of delight.

Vines curl and twist in a jubilant dance,
Where dreams take shape and wishes enhance.
The sky is a canvas of shimmering dreams,
As laughter flows like gentle streams.

Cupids and sprites play hopscotch in air,
In gardens where wonders bloom without care.
Soft winds carry secrets, both old and new,
As magic surrounds in a shimmering hue.

From toadstool thrones to sparkling streams,
Where nothing is ever quite as it seems.
In glades of enchantment, we find our way,
Through the drifts of whimsy, where fairies sway.

A merry-go-round of peculiar sights,
Surrounds the heart on enchanted nights.
In this realm of whimsy, all troubles cease,
As laughter and wonder weave threads of peace.

Dreaming Through a Tangle of Green

Through twisting paths in a tangle of green,
A world of secrets lies, yet unseen.
Leaves murmur stories of days gone by,
As whispers of nature echo a sigh.

Beneath the branches where shadows meet,
Each step unfolds a tale bittersweet.
A dragonfly hovers, a wink in its flight,
In the lush canopy, where dreams take flight.

Sunbeams filter through in a golden haze,
Lighting up wonders in a delicate daze.
With every rustle and gentle breeze,
The heart finds its rhythm among the trees.

Where ferns curl softly and streams softly flow,
The essence of magic begins to grow.
In nature's embrace where dreams entwine,
We wander in wonder, our hearts align.

Through a tangle of green, let us drift and roam,
In fields of enchantment, we find our home.
Where dreams awaken to the softest call,
In nature's embrace, there is magic for all.

Chasing Phantoms in the Mist

In the gloom where shadows play,
Whispers linger, night turns gray.
Figures dance in misty glades,
Carried forth on twilight's blades.

Footsteps echo, soft and near,
Calling forth the long-lost dear.
Through the fog where secrets sigh,
Dreams emerge, but fade and fly.

Moonlit streams, a silver guide,
Haunting tales that twist and slide.
Searching for what once was clear,
Chasing phantoms, drawing near.

Time unwinds, a fragile thread,
Paths entwined where others tread.
Every sigh a tale now spun,
Chasing shadows, lost yet won.

Into the depths, we dare to roam,
In the mist, we find a home.
Where the hearts, once lost, shall meet,
Chasing phantoms, bittersweet.

Sylphs' Secrets in the Twilight

Beneath the boughs where fairies dwell,
Whispers weave a soothing spell.
Sylphs adorn the evening's glow,
Secrets shimmer, soft and low.

In twilight's arms, they dance in grace,
Gentle winds, a warm embrace.
Nestled close in nature's throng,
Harmony, where dreams belong.

Silver leaves, a shimmering hue,
Guard the tales of old and new.
Fleeting forms in dusk's delight,
Sylphs' secrets breathe the night.

Stars awaken, twinkling bright,
Guiding whispers, pure as light.
With every breeze, the stories blend,
Sylphs' secrets never end.

In the twilight, hearts unite,
Held by magic, pure and bright.
In the shadows, dreams take flight,
Sylphs' secrets dance in night.

Ethereal Traces Through Verdant Halls

Through verdant halls where spirits glide,
Echoes of the past abide.
In every leaf, a story stowed,
Ethereal traces gently flowed.

Winding paths of emerald hue,
Whispered dreams, both old and new.
Footfalls light on mossy ground,
In this realm, lost souls are found.

Flickers of light, like stars so bright,
Guide the way in fading light.
In the stillness, wisdom calls,
Linger here in verdant halls.

Murmurs weave through ancient trees,
Carrying the softest breeze.
Guided by the roots so deep,
Ethereal traces lull to sleep.

In twilight's grip, the moment stays,
Where magic glows and laughter plays.
Through verdant halls, our spirits soar,
Ethereal traces, forevermore.

Luminescent Trails by the Faerie Ring

In moonlight's grace, a circle glows,
Where whispered magic ebbs and flows.
Faeries dance on twilight's seam,
Luminescent trails, like dreams.

Beneath the stars, their laughter sings,
Secrets borne on silken wings.
Every twinkle tells a tale,
Of fleeting joy in evening's veil.

Dewdrops sparkle on the leaves,
Weaving trust, tricking thieves.
In this ring of light and song,
We find where all hearts belong.

Gathered close, the world feels right,
With every heart, a spark ignites.
In the dance where shadows cling,
Luminescent trails the faeries bring.

As dawn approaches, dreams take flight,
In fading glow of starlit night.
By the ring, we waltz our way,
Luminescent trails forever stay.

Veils of Light in the Enigma Forest

In the forest where shadows play,
Veils of light dance and sway,
Whispering trees, secrets to keep,
Guiding the lost, luring the deep.

Moonlight glimmers on ancient stone,
Echoes of magic, softly shone,
Each flicker tells tales long gone,
In the heart of night, a spell is drawn.

Chasing shadows, the wanderers roam,
Under the starlight, they find a home,
With laughter and wonder, the hours unfold,
In the embrace of the forest, mysteries told.

Upon the breeze, a sweet refrain,
Notes of enchantment, soft as the rain,
Veils of light weave through the night,
Guiding the way, a gentle sight.

In the stillness, dreams take flight,
Wrapped in whispers, bathed in light,
The enigma unfolds, as dawn draws near,
With every heartbeat, the magic is clear.

Spirits Serenade in the Shaded Glade

In the glade where shadows weave,
Spirits gather, none deceive,
Whispers float on the cool, crisp air,
Songs of memories linger there.

Sunlight dapples through the trees,
Filling the glade with gentle ease,
A symphony of all that's past,
Echoes of laughter, forever cast.

Ancient beings, with eyes aglow,
Sing of tales we long to know,
With each note, our hearts align,
In harmony, the worlds entwine.

Beneath the canopy, dreams are spun,
Two worlds dance, as one, as one,
A serenade of heart and soul,
Enveloped in twilight, stirring and whole.

As dusk descends, the spirits fade,
But in our hearts, their songs invade,
Carried along by winds of time,
In the shaded glade, a lasting rhyme.

Glistening Veils Above Enchanted Paths

Above the paths where magpies sing,
Glistening veils take to the wing,
Flashes of light, like dreams in flight,
Mark the moments when day meets night.

Golden threads in the air do sway,
Guiding travelers on their way,
Each shimmer a promise, softly made,
In the heart of the woods, a magic cascade.

Tread gently where the fairies tread,
Follow the whispers of those long dead,
Through glen and grove, the lanterns gleam,
Woven memories, like threads in a dream.

When shadows gather, the veils grow thin,
Opening doors where stories begin,
Time holds its breath, as secrets unfold,
In glistening veils, the wonder behold.

With every step on enchanted trails,
The heart beats loudly in magic sails,
Above the paths where spirits roam,
In the glistening veils, we find our home.

Trails of Light on Mossy Floors

On mossy floors where silence breathes,
Trails of light weave and wreathes,
Guiding footsteps through the night,
Leading dreams to the morning light.

Under boughs where shadows lie,
Dancing whispers, a soft lullaby,
Every leaf a story told,
In patterns of silver and shades of gold.

Paths of glimmer, shadows cast,
Echoes of futures and whispers of past,
In the woods where the moon shines bright,
Heartbeats quicken at the sight.

With every turn, a new chance blooms,
Among the ferns and fragrant plumes,
Nature sings in a tender tone,
In trails of light, we find our own.

As dawn approaches, colors rise,
The day awakes with serene surprise,
On mossy floors where we tread once more,
In trails of light, forever explore.

Flickering Shadows in the Elysian Meadow

In the meadow where whispers dwell,
Flickering shadows weave their spell.
Moonlight kisses the grass so low,
A dance of secrets, soft and slow.

Beneath the trees, the night birds call,
In twilight's embrace, we surrender all.
The stars above twinkle with glee,
Holding tales of magic, wild and free.

The breeze carries scents of dreams untold,
As the secrets of ages start to unfold.
In the heart of the night, our spirits soar,
In this enchanted place, forevermore.

With every flicker, a memory glows,
In the Elysian meadow, where wonder flows.
A tapestry woven of whispers and sighs,
Where the heart learns to dance and the soul learns to fly.

Celestial Dances Among the Foliage

In twilight's embrace, a waltz begins,
Celestial dancers with shimmering fins.
They glide through the leaves with grace so rare,
Spinning tales in the cool night air.

The foliage rustles with laughter and cheer,
As starlight descends, drawing near.
With each twirl and each gentle sway,
The world around them fades away.

In the shadows, their secrets entwine,
Among the branches, where hearts align.
The night whispers stories, ancient and wise,
As dreams take flight under velvet skies.

With a flick of a wrist, the cosmos brightens,
Awakening magic that silently heightens.
In this realm of the wild, we find our home,
Among celestial dances, forever to roam.

Glowing Petals in the Gloom

Amidst the darkness, they softly gleam,
Glowing petals, like whispers in dream.
Each hue a promise, a story they tell,
Casting light where the shadows fell.

In the stillness, their warmth does spread,
Chasing away the fears we dread.
Like lanterns aglow in the deepening night,
Illuminating paths with their gentle light.

Each fluttering petal a spark of hope,
Guiding the lost, helping them cope.
With beauty that blooms in the heart's embrace,
They reveal the magic in every space.

In the gloom, where darkness tries to creep,
These glowing petals, their watch they keep.
A reminder that even the night can shine,
If we look closely, the stars align.

Haunting Hues of the Mysterious Vale

In the vale where shadows twist and turn,
Haunting hues flicker, beckoning to learn.
Mist lingers softly, hiding the way,
Inviting those brave enough to stay.

With every breath, the whispers grow loud,
Secrets of old wrapped in a shroud.
Colors blend in a ghostly dance,
Drawing dreamers into a trance.

The wind carries tales of sorrow and glee,
Of lovers lost, and those who flee.
In twilight's grasp, where time stands still,
The vale holds magic that bends to will.

As moonlight paints the world in gray,
The hues reveal what shadows convey.
In the mystery of the vale, we find
The haunting beauty that lingers behind.

Veiled Dances in the Emerald Depths

In the forest's heart, shadows twine,
Beneath the leaves, secrets align.
Whispers soft as the twilight breeze,
Veiled dances stir beneath the trees.

Moonlight filters through branches high,
Casting dreams where fairies fly.
In pools of jade, reflections play,
A tapestry of night and day.

Ancient songs on the wind are spun,
Echoes of battles long since won.
Each flicker of light, a story told,
In emerald depths, the brave and bold.

Leaves shimmer, a spellbound display,
Magic lingers, come what may.
With every rustle, a tale unfurls,
In this realm where enchantment swirls.

So tread softly on this sacred ground,
Where the unseen and dreams abound.
For in these woods, boundless and free,
Veiled dances await, just don't flee.

Enchanted Flickers Amidst Mossy Rocks

Among the stones, where shadows play,
Glowing sparks thread night and day.
Each flicker whispers a spell so bright,
A dance of magic wrapped in light.

Mossy cushions cradle tired feet,
Nature's embrace, a soft heart beat.
Rivulets babble with laughter sweet,
In this enchanted, secret retreat.

The air is thick with stories past,
Of laughter shared, of spells cast.
Glimmers dart like a fleeting dream,
In this realm, nothing's what it seems.

Beneath the stars, where wishes soar,
Hope entwines with ancient lore.
Among the flickers, hearts ignite,
In radiant realms, joy takes flight.

So come and seek the magic here,
Amidst the rocks, let go your fear.
For in this haven, wild and free,
Enchanted flickers will always be.

Cosmic Whispers in Sylvan Silence

In silence deep, the cosmos hums,
A melody where night succumbs.
Stars twinkle in a velvet sea,
Whispers of fate, wild and free.

Beneath the boughs of ancient trees,
The night air stirs with gentle ease.
Every breath, a universe unfurls,
In the hush of night, time twirls.

Hidden worlds in the shadows dance,
In every heartbeat, a fleeting chance.
Celestial songs weave through the air,
Cosmic echoes, a soft prayer.

With each flicker of distant light,
Dreamers deep in the arms of night.
Here, the earth and stars conspire,
To ignite the heart with celestial fire.

So linger long in this still embrace,
Where the stars and trees hold grace.
In the silence, hear the call,
Cosmic whispers belong to all.

Hazy Fancies Beneath the Elder Moon

Beneath the moon, silver and bright,
Hazy fancies take flight.
In the mist, dreams softly creep,
Through the shadows, secrets seep.

Elders whisper tales of old,
Of lovers lost and stories told.
In this glimmering twilight glow,
Magic stirs, the night to sow.

Fireflies dance in jubilant glee,
Awakening the magic in me.
Each flicker a promise, a fleeting glance,
In the haze, lost in the trance.

The world dissolves into a sigh,
As wishes wander and softly fly.
In this sacred, storied night,
Hazy fancies bring pure delight.

So wander here in the glow so bright,
Beneath the elder moon's soft light.
For in this moment, wild and free,
Dreams awaken, just like me.

Ethereal Threads in Moonlit Groves

In moonlit groves where shadows play,
The whispers of the night dance bright,
Ethereal threads in silver sway,
Binding dreams to the soft twilight.

Amid the trees, the secrets hum,
With silver leaves that shimmer soft,
A lullaby of whispers come,
As starlit eyes gaze from aloft.

Each breath carries the magic forth,
With glimmers gliding through the air,
Woven tales of wonder's worth,
Embrace the night without a care.

The woodland sings in hushed delight,
While faeries twirl in gleaming stride,
Their laughter weaves through velvet night,
As hearts unite in gentle tide.

So rest your soul 'neath ancient oaks,
Where moonbeams break the dawn's sweet hold,
And in this space, let wonder cloak,
As stories of the night unfold.

Mystical Echoes Beneath Ancient Boughs

Beneath the boughs where shadows dwell,
Mystical echoes rise and fall,
Each murmur spun like a magic spell,
Inviting whispers to enthrall.

The forest breathes with timeless grace,
In every rustle, secrets kept,
An ageless dance time can't erase,
As dreams and shadows softly crept.

With every step, the earth does sigh,
A tapestry of light and shade,
In twilight's grasp, the spirits fly,
In hidden realms where hopes are laid.

The night a canvas, dark yet bright,
Stars sprinkle tales across the sky,
And as your heart takes gentle flight,
The echoes sing a lullaby.

So wander deep, let silence reign,
Where ancient trees embrace your soul,
In nature's heart, release the pain,
And find the magic that makes you whole.

Faint Glows in the Faerie Woods

In faerie woods where shadows weave,
Faint glows shimmer like a sigh,
With every step, the heart believes,
In glimmers soft that twinkle nigh.

The ferns sway gently in the breeze,
While twinkling lights drift through the night,
As whispers stir with such sweet ease,
And stars above lend their soft light.

A tapestry of dreams and lore,
Bestows a magic deep and wide,
As time forgets what came before,
In this enchanted, wondrous tide.

With every pulse, the forest beams,
A symphony of light and sound,
In twilight's grasp, we weave our dreams,
As faerie laughter spins around.

So close your eyes and breathe the air,
Let every worry fade away,
In faerie woods, without a care,
Embrace the magic, come what may.

Celestial Hues of the Hidden Realm

In hidden realms where colors blend,
Celestial hues brush skies of night,
With every stroke, the worlds transcend,
Where stars ignite in pure delight.

The whispers ride on gentle wind,
A chorus soft of worlds unknown,
As waves of light begin to bend,
And weave the patterns swiftly sown.

With every glance, the heavens glow,
A tapestry of dreams unfold,
In twilight's arms, our spirits flow,
As stories timelessly retold.

Upon the path where wonders lie,
The essence of the night awakes,
And as the constellations cry,
The universe a song that breaks.

So dance beneath the sky's embrace,
Where mysteries beckon, bright and clear,
In celestial hues, find your place,
And let your heart dissolve in cheer.

The Dance of Spirits Beneath Ancient Trees

In twilight's grasp, where shadows sway,
The spirits twirl, in soft ballet.
With whispered songs, the breeze does weave,
Their laughter echoes, we scarcely believe.

Beneath the boughs of ancient might,
They dance in moonbeams, pure and light.
Footfalls muted on the ground,
In this secret world, joy is found.

The leaves commune in rustling tones,
As magic swirls among the stones.
With every flicker, stars ignite,
A tapestry of pure delight.

A fleeting glimpse, a haunting sound,
Bound by the night, they spin around.
Lost to the hours, they leave no trace,
Yet in our hearts, they find their place.

When dawn breaks forth, they fade away,
Yet linger softly in light's array.
For in our dreams, their dance remains,
A cherished spark in heart's domains.

Radiant Echoes in the Forest's Heart

In forests deep, where shadows play,
The echoes sing, a soft ballet.
With every rustle, stories bloom,
Awakening magic, dispelling gloom.

The sunlight weaves through emerald leaves,
A golden thread that gently cleaves.
Each sound a whisper, each glance a gift,
The heart of the woods, where spirits lift.

In tranquil pools, reflections dance,
Mysteries thrumming in a trance.
The silence hums with ancient lore,
Of those who wandered, and those before.

A songbird's melody softly breaks,
The stillness shatters, the woodland shakes.
Every note like a sparkling gem,
Resonates deep within the stem.

To wander here is to roam through time,
Among the stories in rhythm and rhyme.
In every nook, the echoes call,
In the forest's heart, we find it all.

Glimmering Traces of a Timeless Encounter

In twilight's weave, where dreams take flight,
Glimmers emerge from the cradle of night.
Each twinkling hint, a tale untold,
Whispers of beings, both brave and bold.

Through silver mist, they drift and glide,
A dance of shadows, side by side.
Their laughter mingles with the sighing breeze,
An orchestra played among the trees.

Fleeting moments, grasped yet gone,
Leaving behind a cryptic song.
Each spark awakens long-forgotten sights,
Of cherished days and enchanted nights.

In glimmering paths, we chase the light,
Tracing the echoes of pure delight.
For in each flicker, there's a trace,
Of timeless wonder we dare embrace.

The heart holds fast to these fleeting dreams,
Forever intertwined, or so it seems.
In glimmering traces, we're never apart,
For every encounter leaves its mark.

The Lure of Light in Ethereal Realms

In realms unknown, where shadows dance,
The lure of light, a spectral chance.
With every flicker, hearts are drawn,
To wander paths from dusk till dawn.

Softly glowing, the spirits rise,
Bright as stars in velvet skies.
Their gentle pull, a calling song,
Inviting souls to journey along.

Through veils of mist and starlit streams,
In every corner, hope redeems.
A shiver of magic, a brush with fate,
In ethereal realms, we contemplate.

With whispered dreams and wishes clear,
The light beckons, we draw near.
In every shadow, the promise gleams,
A world alive with shimmering dreams.

And when we dance in this radiant glow,
A fusion of light and love shall flow.
For in these realms, forever we'll stay,
Where the lure of light guides us on our way.

Enchanted Breezes Through Leafy Lanes

In the dappled light where shadows play,
Whispers of magic drift softly away.
Leaves murmur secrets, their stories unfold,
Breezes like laughter, a comfort from old.

Glistening paths of emerald hue,
Dance with the sparkles of morning dew.
Nature's embrace in each gentle sigh,
Awakens the spirit, as time flutters by.

With every flutter of wings overhead,
Sprightly sprites weave where few dare to tread.
Laughter and warmth linger in the air,
As enchantments weave through the sun-dappled fair.

Among the tall oaks, mysteries lurk,
Roots intertwine in a wondrous work.
Echoes of footfalls from ages long past,
Whisper of dreams in the shadows they cast.

In leaf-strewn paths where the wild roses grow,
The heart finds solace, as soft breezes blow.
Under the boughs where the twilight prevails,
Magic awakens in enchanted trails.

Ghostly Glimpses of the Forgotten Realm

In the twilight's shroud, shadows begin,
Echoes of laughter from where they've been.
Whispers of secrets and tales of regret,
Glimmers of hope in the misty sunset.

Across the old stones, a shimmer of light,
Figures emerge from the depths of night.
With a flicker of dreams and a sigh of the past,
Ghostly reflections in silence are cast.

They dance on the breeze, both fleeting and fair,
Hoping to linger a moment to share.
Fables forgotten, now woven in air,
Haunting the edges, forever laid bare.

Through winding corridors of time's gentle hand,
They trace the lost stories of this shadowed land.
Visions forgotten, like stars in the dark,
Yearning for memory, a flickering spark.

Though the world may turn and the seasons will change,
Their essence remains, timeless and strange.
In the heart of the night, they softly still dwell,
Guardians of stories too precious to tell.

Moonbeams and Moonshadow Whispers

When the moon climbs high in a silvered sky,
Dreams come alive, as the stars twinkle by.
Beneath the soft glow, the world sings anew,
Moonbeams and shadows weave tales just for you.

Glimmers of silver on the rippling stream,
Whispers of wishes escape like a dream.
In the still of the night, where the cool breezes blow,
Magic awakens, both gentle and slow.

Each moment a treasure that time can't confine,
As moonlight dances on petals divine.
Every breath a promise of wonder to find,
In the hush of the night, where thoughts intertwine.

Voices of nightingales float on the air,
Songs of enchantment, a world free from care.
Under the branches, serenity reigns,
Wrapped in the solace that starlight contains.

So linger a while in this tranquil embrace,
Let moonshadow whispers guide you at pace.
The night holds a secret, both soft and profound,
In moonbeams' soft glow, pure magic is found.

Traces of the Elven Nightfall

As the sun bids farewell to the edge of the glade,
Elven whispers echo, in twilight arrayed.
Starlight begins, like a dance in the air,
Traces of nightfall, both lovely and rare.

Delicate breezes caress the tall grass,
In the hush of the evening, where shadows amass.
With a flick of their hands, they beckon the night,
Illuminating dreams with a shimmering light.

Through a canopy woven of silvers and gold,
Stories of old that the starlight has told.
Each flicker a promise of journeys untaken,
In the depths of the woods, where the ancient are
wakened.

Dance lightly through realms where whispers ignite,
Guided by glowworms, they shimmer and write.
Elven echoes slip through the veil of the dark,
Leaving behind just a soft, ethereal mark.

So remember their songs when the darkness descends,
And the light of the stars brings the magic it lends.
For in every moonbeam and fleeting delight,
The traces of elven enchantments take flight.

Hidden Glows of the Verdant Realm

In whispers soft the green leaves sway,
Secrets held in shadows play,
Where laughter dances on the breeze,
And dreams are carried through the trees.

The brook hums low a gentle tune,
Beneath the watchful silver moon,
A carpet lush where fairies tread,
With petals bright their paths are spread.

Mossy stones in emerald beds,
A realm where light and magic spreads,
In every corner life ignites,
In hidden glows of starry nights.

The breeze tells tales of ancient lore,
Of woodland sprites and spirits' store,
In whispering trees the old ones dwell,
Guarding secrets, weaving spells.

So venture forth, where wonders dwell,
In verdant realms, beneath the spell,
Where nature's heart beats wild and free,
In hidden glows of mystery.

Specters of Dawn in the Glimmering Grove

As morning breaks, the shadows flee,
Specters dance with glee,
In glimmering light the dew drops gleam,
Awakening life in a golden dream.

The whispering winds on branches play,
Singing of night and the close of day,
Where echoes of laughter softly sigh,
And sparkles of magic touch the sky.

In every nook a story hides,
Within the grove where hope abides,
With glimmers faint that guide the way,
Through paths of dawn, both bright and gray.

Beneath the boughs, a calm unfolds,
A symphony of tales retold,
In the glimmering light, spirits roam,
Crafting dreams that beckon home.

So linger long where shadows weave,
In the dawning light, take heed,
For specters of dawn, with gentle grace,
Will guide you to a sacred place.

Enigmatic Reflections of the Dreamscape

In twilight's hush, the dreamscape calls,
Where time dissolves and silence falls,
Reflections bright in twilight's glow,
Enigmas dance, and visions flow.

A tapestry of stars unfurled,
Whispers weave through a slumbering world,
In shadows dark, the secrets keep,
As dreams and thoughts drift into sleep.

With each soft sigh, the visions blend,
In a realm where beginnings and endings bend,
Where every thought takes flight on wings,
And the heart remembers what it sings.

Through silence deep, the echoes twine,
In the mirrored depths of a thought divine,
Where reflections shimmer like ancient lore,
And every whisper opens a door.

So wander there, where dreams entwine,
In the secret place where shadows shine,
For within the depths of this mystic space,
Lie enigmatic reflections of grace.

Wisped Lanterns Beneath the Elder Trees

In twilight's shroud, the lanterns glow,
Like fireflies in a gentle flow,
Beneath the elder trees they dance,
Charming hearts with a fleeting glance.

Their whispers echo through the night,
Guiding wanderers with soft light,
In the underbrush, secrets sigh,
As dreams emerge and shadows fly.

Along the path where whispers weave,
The lanterns twinkle, and shadows cleave,
Each flicker tells a tale untold,
Of ages past and futures bold.

With every step on silken dew,
The world transforms, and wonders brew,
In the cradle of the towering trees,
Where wisped lanterns sway with ease.

So seek the light in twilight's veil,
Where time stands still and dreams unveil,
Beneath the elder trees, behold,
The magic of the night unfolds.

Mystical Mists in Enchanted Glades

In twilight's grasp, the mists arise,
A dance of whispers, beauty lies.
Through emerald leaves, the secrets spill,
Where magic treads with gentle thrill.

Fairies flit on silver wings,
Their laughter rings as moonlight sings.
In shimmering pools, reflections gleam,
As starlit dreams weave through the stream.

The ancient trees with knowing sighs,
Stand sentinel 'neath twilight skies.
They guard the tales of ages past,
In leafy whispers, shadows cast.

The creature's rustle in the dark,
A fleeting glimpse, a sudden spark.
With every breath, the forest hums,
As nature's heartbeats softly drums.

Enchanted glades, a world apart,
Where magic lingers, steals the heart.
Embodying dreams in misty shrouds,
In harmony with stars, so proud.

Flickering Shadows Beneath Ancient Boughs

Beneath the boughs, where quiet dwells,
Flickering shadows weave their spells.
The moonlight streams through branches wide,
In whispered tones, the night confides.

The wind it stirs, a waltz of leaves,
As mystery dances, softly weaves.
Each rustle speaks of tales untold,
Of heroes brave and hearts of gold.

In secret nooks, the secrets hide,
Awaiting those with hearts aligned.
With bated breath, enchantments cast,
In echoing sighs of legends past.

Through tangled roots and moonlit paths,
The forest breathes, its heart it hath.
Beneath the stars, the shadows play,
In timeless waltz, they drift away.

With every step, the stories bloom,
In ancient woods, where spirits loom.
Embrace the night, let wonders flow,
For magic thrums where shadows grow.

Whispers of Twilight in Realm of Dreams

In twilight's glow, the silence sighs,
Beneath the stars, where magic lies.
A realm of dreams, both deep and wide,
Where fantasies and hopes abide.

The moonlight glimmers on azure streams,
As shadows paint the night with dreams.
In secret gardens, wishes bloom,
Awakening the heart with tune.

The air is thick with whispers sweet,
As slumbered souls begin to meet.
In realms unseen, their spirits soar,
Through dreamscape doors, they wander more.

With every breath, the night unfolds,
A tapestry of dreams retold.
In harmony with stars above,
The whispers weave a tale of love.

Embrace the night, surrender fears,
For in this realm, the heart appears.
In wondrous worlds where dreams ignite,
Awaits the magic of the night.

Gossamer Threads in the Moonlit Grove

In moonlit groves, where shadows twine,
Gossamer threads of magic shine.
With silken grace, the night unfolds,
A tapestry of stories told.

Beneath the stars, the creatures weave,
A dance of heart where few believe.
Through whispered vows, enchanting charms,
The night wraps all in tender arms.

Dew-kissed petals gleam and sway,
As dreams entwine in soft ballet.
In every breath, the magic swirls,
A dance of fate as twilight twirls.

The ancient trees listen and sway,
Guarding secrets of the day.
In this embrace, the soul finds peace,
As time slips by and dreams increase.

With gossamer threads, the night does weave,
A world of wonder, hearts believe.
In moonlit groves, where spirits roam,
Each whispered word can lead you home.

Vignettes of Magic in Whispering Woods

In the woods where shadows play,
Whispers of old stories sway.
Moonlit paths where fairies dwell,
Every leaf holds a secret spell.

Glimmers of light twinkle on high,
As owls call and suddenly fly.
Branches twist and turn with grace,
Time slows down in this enchanted space.

With every step, the magic thrums,
Echoes of laughter softly hums.
Nature sings in a gentle tune,
Beneath the watchful gaze of the moon.

Sprightly spirits dance in the air,
Twists of fate weave dreams rare.
Here, the world feels wide and free,
In this forest, there's bliss to see.

As dawn breaks, the night recedes,
Every heart feels the forest's needs.
Magic lingers, a sweet embrace,
In the whispering woods, find your place.

Whispers of Twilight Dreams

As twilight falls, the stars awake,
Mysteries linger in the still lake.
A hush embraces the cooling air,
While shadows weave without a care.

In this hush, echoes begin to rise,
The soft gazes of hidden eyes.
Dreams whisper secrets to the night,
Bathed in the silver moonlight's light.

Petals unfurl in colors bright,
As night creatures stir, ready for flight.
Through the thickets, soft sounds glide,
Whispers of magic will not abide.

Glistening dew on grass blade tips,
Every moment, a soft eclipse.
In this world, where wishes blend,
The twilight whispers never end.

Let your heart be light, be bold,
As tales of wonder begin to unfold.
With each secret the night does share,
Magic wraps around like a whispered prayer.

Glimmers in the Enchanted Glade

Beneath the boughs of emerald green,
Glimmers of magic can be seen.
Softly the brook begins to sing,
In the glade where fairies take wing.

Golden sunbeams weave through trees,
Greeting the morning with a gentle breeze.
Mushrooms dance in circles small,
While shadows lengthen, embracing all.

Each petal, a story waiting to bloom,
Echoing softly in this fragrant room.
Rustling leaves in symphonic play,
Guide all wanderers who stray.

Magic stirs in the heart of the glade,
Dreams unfurl, as night will fade.
With every step, the veil grows thin,
In this haven, let the magic in.

So linger a while, let wonder grow,
In the enchanted glade, where hearts aglow.
Each glimmer a reminder, pure and sweet,
Of the beauty found in the dreams we meet.

Shadows Dance on Sylvan Paths

In the hush of twilight's embrace,
Shadows gather, a mystical grace.
Trees murmur secrets with every sigh,
As moonbeams flicker in the night sky.

Along the path where whispers roam,
Nature sings, calling you home.
The silver bark glimmers, aglow,
As twilight's magic begins to flow.

A soft breeze carries tales untold,
Of ancient woods and treasures bold.
In these shadows, hearts intertwine,
In sylvan dreams, life feels divine.

Gnarled roots weave through soft, sweet earth,
Every step a promise, a rebirth.
Here in the woodlands, find your song,
In the dance of twilight, you belong.

Let the shadows guide your way,
With whispers of magic night and day.
In these paths where wonder thrives,
Feel the pulse of ancient lives.

www.ingramcontent.com/pod-product-compliance
Ingram Content Group UK Ltd.
Pitfield, Milton Keynes, MK11 3LW, UK
UKHW021325280125
4330UKWH00005B/404